# The Frog Who Thought He

Written by Roger Vaughan Carr

Illustrated by Craig Smith

Kevin lived in a horse trough near a fairground. He spent all his days swimming happily from one end of the trough to the other.

Well, almost all his days. Whenever a horse came for a drink, Kevin stopped swimming and looked up.

"Horses are beautiful animals," he thought. "If I didn't have to live in water I'd **be** a horse."

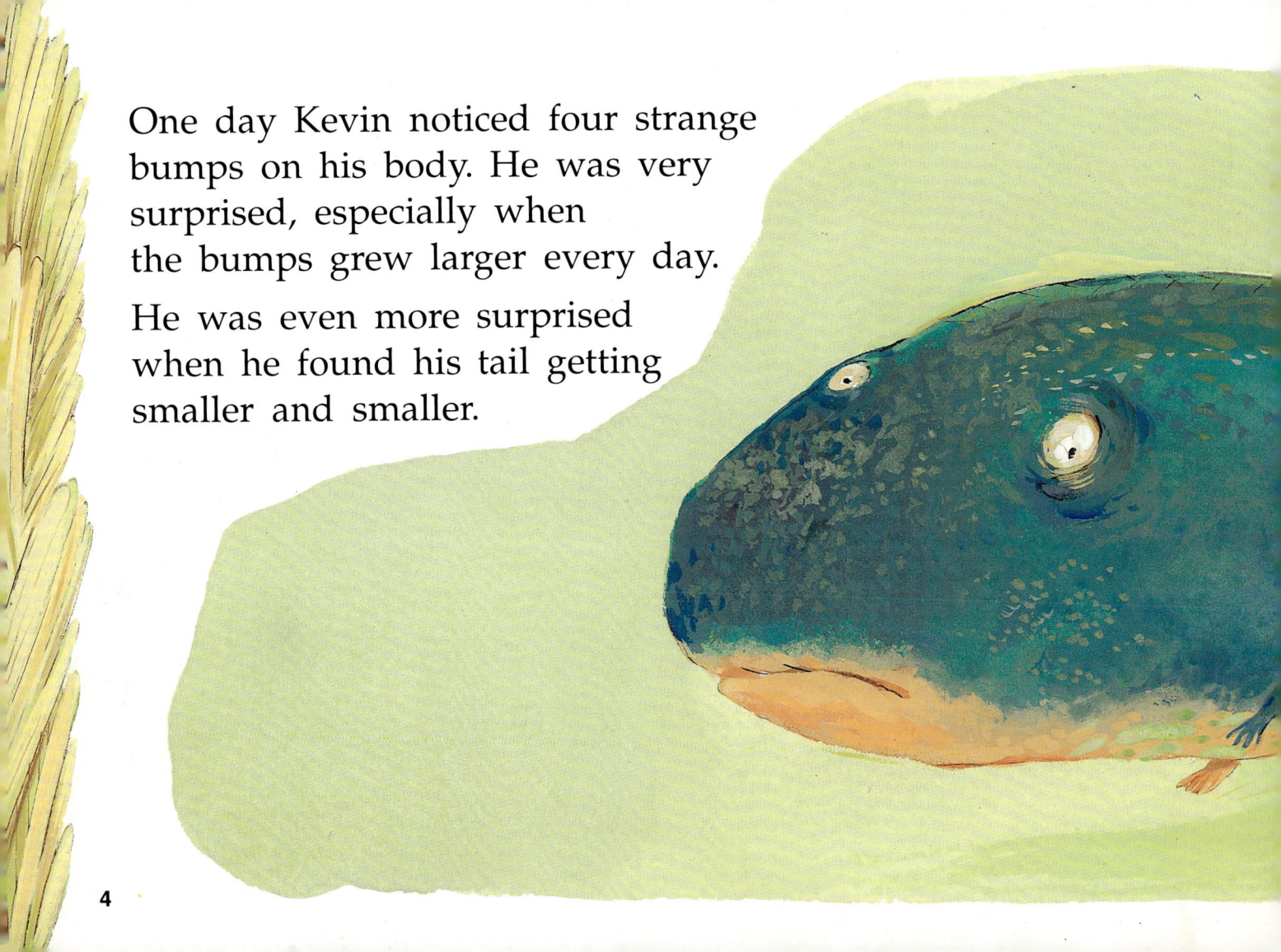

One day Kevin noticed four strange bumps on his body. He was very surprised, especially when the bumps grew larger every day.

He was even more surprised when he found his tail getting smaller and smaller.

"Something strange is happening," Kevin thought to himself.

"Why am I changing? And what am I changing into?"

Kevin looked very closely at the bumps on his body. "Perhaps I'm growing legs," he thought in amazement.

Suddenly he stopped swimming.

"I know what's happening to me! I'm changing into a horse!" he bubbled.

"Me! A horse!"

Kevin pushed his face out of the water and tried a small sniff of the air. Wow! He could breathe! He didn't have to live in the water any more.

"Yippee!" Kevin croaked.
"Now I'm sure I'm a horse."

He swam to the edge of the trough, caught hold of the side, and pulled himself up onto the rim.

A horse was just arriving for a drink.

"Hi, beautiful!" croaked Kevin.

But the horse didn't take any notice. It just finished drinking and then trotted away.

"Wait!" Kevin croaked. He dropped over the side of the trough and tried to trot after the horse — but he just fell over.

A big green frog hopped out from under the trough.

"Hi, junior," he croaked.
"Welcome to the great wide world."

"What are you?" asked Kevin.

"A frog, of course, just like you."

"I'm not a frog," croaked Kevin.
"I'm a horse."

Kevin tried to trot away,
but he fell flat on his face.

"Glup, glup, glup!" the big frog laughed.
"Take my word for it, junior. You are a frog,
and you'd better learn to hop."

He hopped away from the trough
to show Kevin what he meant.

"That's a silly way to move around," said Kevin.
"Horses like me can trot and gallop."
He tried to gallop to show the big frog what he meant, but he fell over again.

"You won't get far doing that," the big frog croaked.
"Take my advice and learn to hop."

"But I'm a **horse**!" Kevin croaked angrily.
He tried to trot and fell over again.
"I'm a horse, I tell you."

All day long, Kevin tried to trot and gallop. But he just couldn't do it. When the big frog hopped out from under the trough again, he saw that poor Kevin was exhausted.

"You don't look very well, junior," he croaked. "Hop on my back and I'll show you something."

Kevin was too tired to argue. He crawled onto the big frog's back and hung on.

With Kevin on his back, the big frog hopped toward the bright lights of the fairground.

He hopped under the fence, and he hopped past one ride after another.

He didn't stop until he reached the merry-go-round.

"Look, junior, do you see those horses?" asked the big frog. Kevin heard the cheerful music and looked at the merry-go-round. He slid off the frog's back.

"There's a horse that's green like me!" he croaked in excitement.

"That's right," said the big frog.
"And do you see how he moves?
Up and down. Up and down.
He doesn't try to trot or gallop."

Kevin watched the green horse as it went up and down, up and down, in time with the music.

Kevin hopped. "Like that?" he asked.

"Just like that," the big frog agreed.

"Yippee!" Kevin croaked, and he hopped up and down some more.

"Now you'll be able to take care of yourself," croaked the big frog.

"Yippee!" Kevin croaked again. "Thank you, frog."

Kevin set off right away.

"I'm a green up-and-down horse," he croaked happily. "Up and down, up and down, up and down."

The big frog watched Kevin go. "He's a crazy kid," he muttered. "Still, if he's happy that way, why should I tell him that he's hopping just like any other frog?"

"Yippee!" Kevin croaked.
"Ordinary horses trot and gallop. Special green horses like me go up and down, up and down, up and down . . ."

When Kevin got home
he sat down and smiled.
"I like being a horse,"
he said.